• HISTORY FROM PHOTOGRAPHS •
Food

Kath Cox and Pat Hughes

Wayland

♦ HISTORY FROM PHOTOGRAPHS ♦

Notes for Parents and Teachers

This book provides a flexible teaching resource for Early Years history. Two levels of text are given – a simple version and a more advanced and extended version. The book can be used for:

- Early stage readers at Key Stage 1
- Older readers needing differentiated text
- Non-readers who can use the photographs
- Extending skills of reading non-fiction
- Adults reading aloud to provide a model for non-fiction reading

By comparing photographs from the past and the present, children are able to develop skills of observation, ask questions and discuss ideas. They should begin by identifying the familiar in the modern photographs before moving on to the photographs from the past. The aim is to encourage children to make 'now' and 'then' comparisons.

The use of old photographs not only provides an exciting primary resource for history but, used alongside the modern photographs, aids the discussion of the development of photography. Modern photographs in black and white are included to encourage children to look more closely at the photographs and avoid seeing the past as 'black and white'. All the historical photographs were taken beyond the living memory of children and most have been selected from the Edwardian period between 1900 and 1920. A comprehensive information section for teachers, parents and other adults on pages 29–31 gives details of each of the old photographs, where known, and suggests points to explore and questions to ask children.

Editor: Carron Brown
Designer: Michael Leaman
Production Controller: Carol Stevens
Consultant: Norah Granger

Front cover: Family and friends around the dinner table, 1900s.
Endpapers: Photographers at work at a wedding, 1907.
Title page: Melia's Stores, a general store from the 1900s.

Picture Acknowledgements
The publishers would like to thank the following for allowing their pictures to be used in this book: The Advertising Archives 12, 13; Beamish Museum 19; Mary Evans Picture Library 9; Eye Ubiquitous *cover* (inset) 24; Chris Fairclough 14, 16; Glasgow University Archives 23; Robert Harding 6, 11; Hulton Getty *cover* (main) 7, 8, 21, 25; Image Bank 4; Impact 26; Liverpool City Libraries 5; The Royal Photographic Society, Bath, *endpapers, contents page*; Topham Picture Source 17, 27; Warrington Museum and Art Gallery title page; Wayland Picture Library 15, 18, 20, 22. /Steve White Thomson 10. All artwork is by Barbara Loftus.

First published in 1996 by Wayland Publishers Limited
61 Western Road, Hove, East Sussex BN3 1JD, England

© Copyright 1996 Wayland Publishers Limited

The right of Kath Cox and Pat Hughes to be identified as the authors of this work has been asserted in accordance with the Copyright, Designs and Patents Act 1988.

British Library Cataloguing in publication Data
Cox, Kathleen
Food. – History from Photographs)
1. Food – History – Juvenile literature 2. Dinners and dining – Great Britain – History – Juvenile literature 3. Marketing (Home economics) – Great Britain – History – Juvenile literature
I. Title II. Hughes, Pat, 1933 –
641.3'00941

ISBN 0 7502 1545 3

Typeset in the UK by Michael Leaman Design Partnership
Printed and bound in Great Britain by B. P. C. Paulton Books Ltd.

Contents

Shopping for Food	4
The Greengrocers	6
Supermarkets	8
Delivering the Milk	10
Advertising Food	12
Bread and Cakes	14
Baking	16
Kitchen Equipment	18
Mealtimes	20
Picnics	22
Fast Food	24
Soup Kitchens	26
Picture Glossary	28
Books to Read and Places to Visit	29
Further Information about the Photographs	30
Index	32

A Brownie box camera and case, 1900.

· NOW ·

Jason is helping his mum with the shopping.

They visit the supermarket every two weeks to buy most of their food. If they run out of anything they can buy more food at a corner shop.
Fresh meat, fish, fruit and eggs are sold in supermarkets as well as in smaller food shops.
Some foods are dried, canned, chilled or frozen to make them keep longer.

1900

Most women shopped for food every day.

They visited many different shops to buy food.
Butchers sold meat.
Fishmongers sold fish.
Eggs were bought at a dairy.
Food did not stay fresh for very long so most people only bought small amounts.

This shop sells fruit and vegetables.

It is called a greengrocers.
Greengrocers sell many different kinds of fruit and vegetables.
Some are grown on farms in this country.
Others are brought by plane or boat from warmer countries like Spain.
We can buy the same kinds of fruit and vegetables all the year round.

· 1907 ·

People ate fruit and vegetables.

Most of the produce came from local farms. It was brought to the towns on trains or horse-drawn carts. Different kinds of fruit and vegetables were sold at different times of year.

Supermarkets are large shops.

Supermarkets sell many different types of food.
Shoppers can get all the food they need in one place.
Most of the food is already weighed and wrapped in boxes,
tins or plastic bags.
Customers can choose what they want from the shelves
and put it in baskets or trolleys.
They pay for the food at a checkout.

•1900•

Some large shops sold different foods.

Assistants weighed and wrapped each item.
People sat on stools while they waited to be served.
Customers collected the food they had chosen after they had paid for it at a central till.
Most shops would deliver goods to the customers' homes.

·NOW·

Cath delivers milk to people's houses.

Milk is collected from dairy farms in road tankers.
The road tankers carry the milk to a dairy where it is put in glass bottles. Milk is also stored in cartons and plastic bottles. Today, many different types of milk can be bought.

· 1910 ·

Milk was sold to people in their homes.

It was carried in large churns and put into jugs, cans or bottles.
There was only one type of milk.
People paid when the milk was delivered.
In the countryside, people bought their milk direct from the farms.

This is an advert for sweets.

Adverts try to make people buy certain goods when they go shopping.
Today, there are many adverts for food, drinks and sweets.
This advert is for fruit gums.
Children can choose from many different kinds of sweets and chocolate.

•1900•

This is an old advert for fruit gums.

Children liked eating sweets and chocolate a hundred years ago.
They bought them in sweet shops or at a general store.
Most sweets were not sold in packets or boxes but were sold loose.
The shopkeeper weighed them and put them in cones of brown paper.

· NOW ·

This is a baker's shop.

It sells many kinds of cakes, pies, buns and bread. These are made in the bakery at the back of the shop. Most people buy this type of food rather than make it themselves at home. Supermarkets also sell bread and cakes.

·1892·

People liked to eat cakes.

Only wealthy people could buy food like this from a bakery.
Most women baked their own bread, pies and cakes.
One day each week was set aside as a baking day.

Darren is making some cakes.

The ingredients are wrapped in containers or bags
to keep them fresh and clean.
Today, most food utensils are made of plastic or stainless steel.
These are easy to keep clean.
Food processors and other kitchen appliances
chop and prepare food quickly.

· 1900 ·

Women cooked the food.

Ingredients were sold loose and only wrapped when a customer bought them.
Most food utensils were made of wood, pottery or metal.
Chopping, slicing, grating and mixing were all done by hand.

A microwave cooks food quickly.

Most families also have an oven with a hob for saucepans.
Bread is toasted under a grill or in a toaster.
Electric kettles make it easier to heat water for a cup of tea or coffee.
Fridges keep food cool so that it keeps fresh longer.
Frozen food kept in a freezer can be stored for months.

· 1900 ·

Food was cooked on a range.

A range had an oven for baking or roasting food.
Saucepans were put on a hot plate on top of the range to heat food.
Bread was held in front of the fire in the range to make toast.
Water was heated in a kettle hung above a fire.
Food was kept cool in a larder.

NOW

The boys are eating pizza.

Their favourite meal is pizza and coke.
The boys eat their food while they watch television.
Their parents will eat later when they come in from work.
At the weekend, the family sit down and eat their meals together.

· 1910 ·

This family ate together.

Parents and children usually sat together for their meals.
The table was set with cutlery and crockery.
In many families, children had to eat and drink in silence.

· NOW ·

This group of friends are having a picnic.

They like eating outside when it is hot.
Jan unpacks the picnic basket.
The sandwiches were made at home.
The fruit and drinks were bought at a supermarket.
Coolpacks in the basket keep the food fresh.

•1912•

These ladies had picnics on the beach.

People enjoyed going for picnics.
Rich families took a lot of food on picnics.
It was carried in large wicker baskets with the crockery and cutlery.
Some picnic hampers had a small stove inside to heat water.

NOW

This van sells take-away food.

It is called take-away food because the people who buy it
do not prepare or cook it.
Take-away food is sold from shops and street stalls as well as from vans.
People eat the food in the street or take it home with them.
Fish, chips, hot-dogs and burgers are all take-away foods.

1900

Food was sold on the street.

Traders sold food and drink from trays and stalls. Sherbet water, coffee, pies, fruit and hot chestnuts could be bought on the street.

This is a soup kitchen.

Soup kitchens provide free meals for people
who do not have money to buy food.
Hot food, sandwiches and drinks are made as well as soup.
Most of the people who go to soup kitchens are adults who are homeless.
Today, many people do not have enough food to eat.

· 1900 ·

Children got food from soup kitchens.

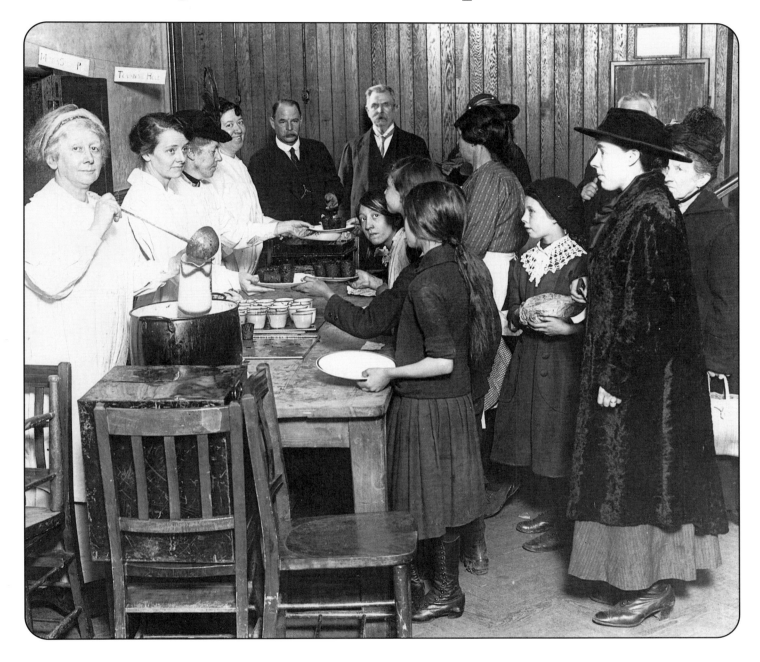

Many families were very poor.
Free food from soup kitchens stopped people from starving.
Most soup kitchens were paid for by charity.

· Picture Glossary ·

 **Butcher** A shopkeeper who sells beef, chicken and other kinds of meat.

 **Horse-drawn carts** Carts pulled by horses. These were used to transport goods before lorries with engines were invented.

 **Churn** A very large can with a lid. It was used to hold milk.

 **Hamper** A large basket with a lid. Used to carry food and drink.

 **Coolpacks** Plastic packs which are put in the freezer to go cold. They are used to hold and store food.

 **Ingredients** Foods that are listed in a recipe. They are mixed together to make the recipe.

 **Crockery** Cups, jugs, bowls and plates that are made from pottery. They are used to hold and store food.

 **Larder** A cold, small room near the kitchen. Food was put there to keep cool.

 **Cutlery** Knives, forks and spoons. They are used to help us eat food.

 **Road tanker** A lorry with a large tank on the back. It is used to carry milk, oil or other liquids.

 **Fishmonger** A shopkeeper who sells many different kinds of fish to be eaten.

 **Utensils** Tools used to prepare food. For example, whisks, sieves and ladles.

Books to Read

A Victorian Kitchen by L. Faulkner (Victorian Life series, Wayland, 1989).
Breakfast by L. Chaney (Turn of the Century series, A & C Black, 1991).
Cooking by R. Thomson (Changing Times series, Franklin Watts, 1992).
Cooking by G. Tanner & T. Wood (History Mysteries series, A & C Black, 1994).
Food We Ate by Stewart Ross (Starting History series, Wayland, 1992).
Shopping by G. Tanner & T. Wood (History Mysteries series, A & C Black, 1994).
Shopping by Stewart Ross (Starting History series, Wayland, 1992).
Shopping for Food by R. Thomson. (Changing Times series, Franklin Watts, 1992).
When I was Young by R. Thomson (Early 20th century series, Franklin Watts, 1993).

The Shire Collection produce a series of short guides, many of which link to food preparation, storage and cooking. A catalogue is available from: Shire Publications, Freepost (AHE135), Princes Risborough, Bucks. HP27 8BR Telephone: 01844 3443301.

Places to Visit

Most museums have collections or displays of objects used in the packaging, storage, preparation, cooking and serving of food. It is worth contacting your local museum to see what it offers. Many historic houses (including some run by the National Trust) provide school parties with opportunities to carry out role play in a turn-of-the-century kitchen.

Acton Scott Historic Working Farm
Wenlock Lodge, Acton Scott
Nr Church Stretton. SY6 6QN

Telephone: 01694 781306/7

Famine Museum
Stockstown, Co Longford, Eire

Museum of Welsh Life
St Fagans, Cardiff. CF5 6XB

Telephone: 01222 569441

Ollerton Mill Centre
and Working Museum
Nr Budleigh, Salterton. EX9 7HG

Telephone: 01395 568521

Shugborough Mansion House
Servants Quarters
Museum of Staffordshire Life and Park
Farm, Milford, Shugborough. Nr Stafford

Telephone: 01889 881388

The Robert Opie Collection
Museum of Advertising and Packaging
Albert Warehouse
Gloucester Docks. GL1 2EH

Telephone: 01452 302309

The Radbrook Culinary Museum
Radbrook College,
Radbrook Road
Shrewsbury. SY3 9BL

Telephone: 01743 232686

Further Information about the Photographs

PHOTOGRAPH ON PAGE 5
St John's Market, Liverpool, 1909.

About this photograph
Food shopping was very different in Edwardian times. There were two main reasons for this. Firstly, preserving food was difficult and so food could not be stored for long. Hence housewives bought little and shopped often. Secondly, some working-class men were paid on a daily basis and so their wives could only buy small amounts each day. For many families even a weekly wage was not sufficient to last the full week, and 'running short' of food was common. Solutions included buying on credit from a corner shop, pawning family possessions and borrowing food from neighbours.

Questions to ask
What types of shops can be seen?
Wat types of food would be sold in these shops?
Why do the shop windows have canopies over them?

Points to explore
Investigate different displays and labelling used in Edwardian shops.
People – clothes, how they travelled to the shops, food they bought.

PHOTOGRAPH ON PAGE 7
Greengrocers, Denham Street, Soho, 1907.

About this photograph
Fruit and vegetables had a much stricter seasonal availability. Some examples of imported fruit can be seen (i.e. grapes and bananas) but these were exceptions. Transport was slow and produce deteriorated rapidly. In the country, families with gardens grew their own fruit and vegetables. Markets were still important as places to buy fruit and vegetables.

Questions to ask
What sort of fruit and vegetables can you see?
What else does the greengrocer sell?

Points to explore
Shop assistants – clothes, duties.
Produce – how it was weighed, wrapped.

PHOTOGRAPH ON PAGE 9
Sainsbury's, c.1900.

About this photograph
Sainsbury's began as a small dairy in the 1870s, and by 1900 had 16 shops, mainly in the London area. The layout shows Sainsbury's house-style. Scales were visible in the shop to reassure customers that they were not being cheated. Customers went to each part of the shop to purchase what they required. An assistant weighed and wrapped the goods and gave the customer a piece of paper with the price on it. Payment at a central till avoided assistants handling both money and food. Wealthy customers placed food orders that would be delivered by the shop or collected by a servant.

Questions to ask
What types of food were sold?
What are the women at the back doing?

Points to explore
Layout of the counter (i.e. equipment, glass shields, storage).

PHOTOGRAPH ON PAGE 11
Selling milk, c. 1910.

About this photograph
Milk came in bottles as well as containers. The milk available was full-cream. The quality of milk sold in the towns had been improved, and was safer than it had been in the late nineteenth century. By 1910, people were aware of the need for a safe, good-quality milk supply. Many food products were sold door-to-door or by street traders. These included bread, fish, muffins and cress. Travelling dealers, called higglers, bought poultry, eggs and vegetables and sold them door-to-door.

Questions to ask
How was the milk kept clean and cool?
What would be the problems of selling milk in this way?

Points to explore
Food delivery – other types of food sold or delivered to households.
Use old photographs to find how food was transported (i.e. push carts, bicycle carts, delivery bicycles, horse-drawn carts).

PHOTOGRAPH ON PAGE 13
Rowntrees advert, c.1900s.

About this photograph
Food and sweet manufacturers soon realized the importance of brightly coloured packaging to make their products look attractive. People began to prefer food in sealed packets so that they could be sure that shop-keepers were not adding low-grade substances (e.g. tree leaves mixed with tea leaves). Sweets such as fruit gums would be packed in boxes or large, glass jars, and bought by weight. They would then be put in cones of brown paper. Children who had money for sweets would usually have bought them from general stores near their homes.

Questions to ask
What flavours would the sweets have been?
How can you tell this advert is aimed at children?

Points to explore
Details of the children in the advert.
Type of sweets available now and in 1900.
Packaging of sweets and chocolates now and in 1900.

PHOTOGRAPH ON PAGE 15
Bread and cakes, 1892.

About this photograph
This is an early example of colour photography. Usually, colour photographs from this time were tinted by hand. This photograph was produced by a line-screen process that used colour dyes on the transparency. The range of bread and cakes shown is indicative of what was available to wealthy customers. Most people baked bread and cakes themselves or had a servant do it for them. Shop-bought items would have been wrapped in paper.

Questions to ask
What different types of bread and cakes can you see?
How do you know this photograph was not taken in a bread shop?
Which of the items can be bought in bakeries today?

Points to explore
Compare the range of bread we have today to that in the 1900s.

PHOTOGRAPH ON PAGE 17	**Baking, c.1910.**

About this photograph
In working-class households, a day was set aside for baking the family's supply of bread, pies and cakes. A day shortly after pay day was often chosen as there was usually money for the ingredients. The types of dry ingredients used were sold loose and wrapped to order. Many of the kitchen utensils used in Edwardian times are very similar to those today. The main differences were the materials. Metal utensils tended to go rusty and required extra cleaning. In poorer areas, it was not unusual to take prepared food to the local bake-house in the morning and collect it cooked on the way home.

Questions to ask
What do you think the woman is making?
Are there any objects that you would find in a kitchen today?

Points to explore
Background objects (i.e. different utensils used for cooking).
Compare storage of food then and now.

PHOTOGRAPH ON PAGE 19	**Kitchen range, c.1900.**

About this photograph
This is an open range, so-called because the fire is directly open to the room and not behind a door. Open ranges were more common in the north where they could heat houses. Pots, pans and kettles were used by being suspended over the fire. Pies, tarts, cakes and bread would be cooked in an oven at the side. Oven heat could be regulated by a damper (next to the irons on this photograph.

Questions to ask
How could food be cooked on this range?
What were some of the difficulties with cooking like this?

Points to explore
Range equipment (i.e. damper, skillet, kettle, pot, tongs, pot hooks).
Compare how food cooked today with 1900.

PHOTOGRAPH ON PAGE 21	**Edwardian family tea, 1910.**

About this photograph
Families usually sat down together for meals. Women without servants had to serve food and drink to her family. In working-class and middle-class households, food was likely to have been home-made. Meals were seen as opportunities to teach manners to the children. In working-class homes, it was usual for the father to receive the best food as his health and strength was vital to the family's income. Meals in wealthy Edwardian households would have been very elaborate with servants preparing and serving food. Children often ate separately, supervised by a nanny.

Questions to ask
What do you think the children are eating and drinking?
What meal do you think this is?

Points to explore
Use non-fiction books to find out about types of food eaten for different meals in Edwardian times.

PHOTOGRAPH ON PAGE 23	**Beach at Gullane, Scotland, 1912.**

About this photograph
Picnics were very popular. For many people a day in the countryside or at the seaside was their only break from work. Developments in public transport meant that this kind of treat became accessible to a wider range of people. Rich family picnics would be a very grand affair with large amounts of elaborate food prepared by servants. This photograph shows a more modest and informal picnic. The sandwiches are in an old tin. Beverages include bottled soft drinks and cocoa made from water kept hot in a flask.

Questions to ask
What do you think the people might be eating and drinking?
Who do you think prepared the picnic?
Why do you think the photograph was taken?

Points to explore
People – age, pose, clothing.
Containers used to transport picnic food between then and now.
Use additional photographs to investigate other examples of picnics (e.g. school & church outings, wealthy family picnics, hunting).

PHOTOGRAPH ON PAGE 25	**Selling sherbet water in Cheapside, c. 1900.**

About this photograph
The sherbet water cost 1/2d a glass. Anyone could sell food or drink. So, standards of hygiene and cleanliness varied. Sometimes, children were sent out to sell home-made food to help add to the family income. Fish and chips were sold in many industrial towns from the 1860s onwards. Not everyone had cooking facilities at home. Take-away food was often the only hot food some people ate.

Questions to ask
Why do you think the boy is drinking in the street?
What type of food is the woman selling?

Points to explore
Street (i.e. vehicles, buildings, street furniture) and people (i.e. clothes).

PHOTOGRAPH ON PAGE 27	**Communal soup kitchen, Hammersmith, 1917.**

About this photograph
The number of adult onlookers suggests that this photograph was posed for a specific purpose. The Edwardian period saw the first steps towards the welfare state. Free meals for under-nourished school children, selective unemployment and health schemes for workers, and minimal pensions for 'deserving' over 70-year-olds all helped to reduce the level of poverty. However, this still excluded many people who existed at subsistence level. For these people healthy diets were impossible and they were often in poor health. The soup kitchen was an immediate response to relieve starvation (e.g. during miners 'strikes and the very poorest areas of the towns).

Questions to ask
What is happening in the photograph?
What food do you think is being served?

Points to explore
Serving the food (i.e. utensils, containers).
Investigate the range of reasons for not having enough food to eat.

· Index ·

(Items that appear in text)

Aa adverts 12, 13

Bb bags 8, 16
bakers 14, 15
basket 8, 22, 23
bottles 10, 11, 13
bread 14, 15, 18, 19
buns 14
burgers 24
butchers 5

Cc cakes 14, 15, 16
cans 11
cartons 10
chips 24
chocolate 12, 13
churns 11
crockery 21, 23
cutlery 21, 23

Dd dairies 5
drinks 12, 22

Ee eggs 4, 5

Ff farms 6, 7, 10, 11
fish 4, 5, 24
fishmongers 5
freezers 18
fridges 18

Gg greengrocers 6

Hh hobs 18
hot-dogs 24
hot plate 19

Ii ingredients 16, 17

Jj jugs 11

Kk kettles 18, 19
kitchens 16, 26, 27

Ll larders 19

Mm meals 20, 21, 26
meat 4, 5
microwaves 18
milk 10, 11

Nn

Oo ovens 18, 19

Pp paper 13
picnics 22, 23
pies 14, 15, 25
pizzas 20

Qq

Rr ranges 19

Ss sandwiches 22, 26
saucepans 18, 19
shops 4, 8, 9, 13, 14, 24
shopping 4, 11
soup 26, 27
sweets 12, 13

Tt tins 8
toast 19
toasters 18

Uu utensils 16, 17

Vv vegetables 6, 7

Ww water 18, 19, 23, 25

Xx

Yy

Zz